Queen Elizabeth II

Susanna Davidson

Designed by Karen Tomlins

History consultant: Hugo Vickers

Family Tree

Queen Victoria (1819-1901)
m. Prince Albert of Saxe-Coburg (1819-61)

Edward VII (1841-1910)
m. Princess Alexandra of Denmark (1844-1925)

George V (1865-1936)
m. Princess Victoria Mary of Teck (1867-1953)

Edward VIII
(1894-1972)
m. Mrs Wallis Simpson (1896-1986)

George VI
(1895-1952)
m. Lady Elizabeth Bowes-Lyon (1900-2002)

Prince Henry
(1900-74)
m. Lady Alice Scott (1901-2004) ↓

Prince George
(1902-42)
m. Princess Marina of Greece & Denmark (1906-68)

Prince John
(1905-19)

Princess Mary
(1897-1965)
m. The 6th Earl of Harewood (1882-1947)

Queen Elizabeth II
(b. 1926)
m. Prince Philip, Duke of Edinburgh (b. 1921)

Princess Margaret
(1930-2002)
m. Antony Armstrong-Jones (b. 1930) (divorced 1978) ↓

Prince Charles
(b. 1948)
m. (1) Lady Diana Spencer (1961-97)
(2) Mrs Camilla Parker Bowles (b. 1947)

Prince Andrew
(b. 1960)
m. Sarah Ferguson (b. 1959) (divorced 1992) ↓

Prince Edward
(b. 1964)
m. Sophie Rhys-Jones (b. 1965) ↓

Princess Anne
(b. 1950)
m. (1) Captain Mark Phillips (b. 1948)
(2) Vice-Admiral Sir Timothy Laurence (b. 1955) ↓

Prince William
(b. 1982)
m. Catherine Middleton (b. 1982)

Prince Harry
(b. 1984)

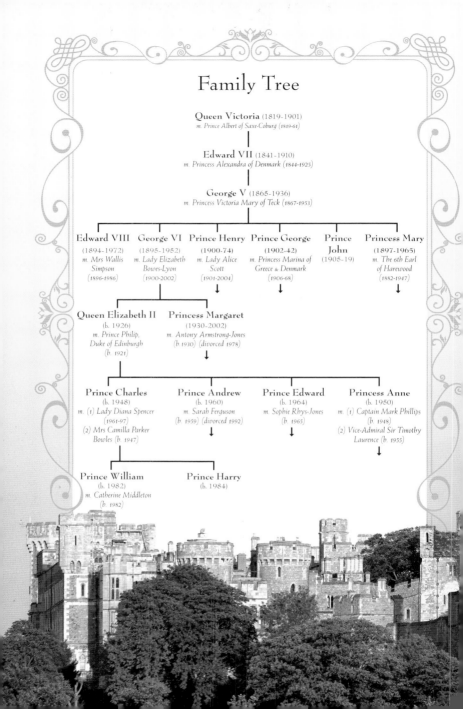

Contents

Chapter 1 Happy families 4

Chapter 2 Heir to the throne 17

Chapter 3 Love & marriage 32

Chapter 4 Head of State 40

Chapter 5 Family strife 49

Chapter 6 A job for life 56

Windsor Castle, one of the Queen's homes, is the oldest and largest occupied castle in the world.

Chapter 1

Happy families

In the early hours of Wednesday April 21, 1926, a royal servant rushed up the stairs and woke the King and Queen to tell them their first granddaughter had been born. "Such relief and joy," Queen Mary wrote in her diary.

No one imagined the newborn princess would one day be queen. Her father, the Duke of York, known as Bertie to his family, was the King's second son. Most people assumed his elder brother, Edward, would become king, and have children of his own.

But this was still a royal baby and Queen Mary was enchanted. "We always wanted a child to make our happiness complete," the Duke of York wrote to his mother a few days later, "and now

The baby Princess Elizabeth with her parents, in her christening gown

that it has at last happened, it seems so wonderful and strange."

A month later, the baby was christened in a gold font at Buckingham Palace, dressed in the heavy satin and lace gown worn by all royal children. She was named Elizabeth Alexandra Mary, after her mother, grandmother and great-grandmother.

The baby princess at ten months, with her nanny, 'Allah' Knight. Allah stayed with Princess Elizabeth for nineteen years, until her death in 1945.

Like most rich and aristocratic families at that time, Elizabeth was looked after by a nanny. Clara Knight, known to the family as Allah, believed strongly in order and discipline. The baby princess followed a strict routine and was wheeled out every morning and evening to take the air.

Elizabeth's mother visited the nursery daily and was devoted to her baby, but royal duty came first. In January 1927, when Elizabeth was just nine months old, her parents were sent on a tour of Australia and New Zealand. "I felt very much leaving on Thursday," wrote her mother, "and the baby was so sweet playing with the buttons on Bertie's uniform, it quite broke me up."

When the Duke and Duchess finally returned, Elizabeth was one year and two months old – she had been separated from her parents for almost half her life. They were reunited at Buckingham Palace. When the Duchess saw the baby in her nurse's arms she rushed forward, crying, "Oh you little darling," kissing and hugging her again and again. Then Elizabeth was taken out onto the balcony and held up to cheering crowds.

The Duke and Duchess of York wave from their balcony, shortly after their return from their royal tour. The Duchess is holding Princess Elizabeth.

The family moved to a new house, 145 Piccadilly, where Elizabeth was to spend the next ten years. It lay just across the park from Buckingham Palace, and had five floors, a library, a ballroom, a conservatory and twenty-five bedrooms, most of which were for the servants. Elizabeth, Allah and the nursery-maid, known as Bobo, had a whole floor to themselves – a world safe and secure from all that went on outside.

From the start, the public was fascinated with the young princess. When a magazine wrote that Elizabeth was usually dressed in yellow, children all over the world started to dress in yellow too.

The princess had chocolates, tea sets, hospital wards and even a slice of Antarctica named after her.

The Yorks became the public image of the happy family – an image that was

Princess Elizabeth, at two years old, with her mother

completed by the birth of a second child, Margaret Rose, in August 1930. It was soon clear that the two sisters were total opposites – Elizabeth was sensible and careful, while Margaret was naughty and amusing. The children's governess, Marion Crawford, always known as Crawfie, described how the conscientious Elizabeth would look after her toy horses, grooming, feeding and watering them, before lining up their brushes and pails outside the nursery each night.

The young princesses play in the garden of their grandparents, the Earl and Countess of Strathmore.

Although four years apart, the sisters were always close, with Elizabeth feeling very protective of Margaret. The Duke of York was determined that Margaret should never feel left out, and made sure she was included in everything her sister did. They were even dressed in the same clothes up until their teenage years. 'Us four', the Duke of York called his family, and they were close-knit and contented.

This photograph shows the royal family at their country home, the Royal Lodge, in Windsor.

Princess Elizabeth stands with her grandparents on Buckingham Palace balcony. You can just see Princess Margaret's head as she peers over the edge.

Elizabeth was close to her grandparents too, particularly the King, George V, who gave her the nickname 'Lilibet'. He also gave Elizabeth her first pony, a Shetland called Peggy, for her fourth birthday.

That same day she walked across the square at Windsor Castle, in a yellow coat trimmed with fur. A band played and she waved at the surging crowds, while the women blew back kisses. In these early years of her life, Elizabeth was learning what it meant to be royal.

Princess Elizabeth sits next to her grandmother, Queen Mary, on their way to a ceremony at St. James's Palace, London. Her mother sits opposite and her aunt, Princess Mary, is beside her.

Elizabeth could see the deference with which people treated the King and Queen, and from the age of three was curtseying to them herself.

From her grandmother, Queen Mary, she learned that there were strict codes of royal conduct. On a trip to a concert, Elizabeth fidgeted so much the Queen asked her if she wanted to go home. "Oh no, Granny," Elizabeth said, "we can't leave before the end. Think of all the people who'll be waiting to see us outside." Queen Mary thought she was being big-headed, and sent her home in disgrace.

In 1935, Elizabeth experienced the grandeur of a royal occasion with her grandfather's Silver Jubilee, a huge event celebrating his twenty-five years on the throne. Elizabeth and her sister, dressed in matching pink, drove through the cheering crowds in an open carriage to St. Paul's Cathedral.

A souvenir card celebrating King George V's Silver Jubilee

The royal carriage can be seen here, leaving Buckingham Palace on the day of the Silver Jubilee.

A crowd looks on as the princesses
arrive at an event in London, in 1936.

The princesses were discovering how different
they were to ordinary people, and it made them
all the more fascinated by them, especially other
children. Their governess, Crawfie, noticed how,
"The little girls used to smile shyly at those they
liked the look of. They would so have loved to
speak to them and make friends, but this was
never encouraged."

Princesses Elizabeth and Margaret enjoy a trip to London Zoo with their governess, Crawfie, in 1938. Elizabeth is third from the left, Margaret is second from the right.

Crawfie began to try to take them on trips into the 'ordinary world' but this soon proved too difficult. On one occasion they went by underground to a canteen. Elizabeth left her pot of tea behind on the counter and was shouted at by the woman serving. But they were soon recognized, and attracted so much attention their detective had to call up a car to take them back, so they could escape from the gathering crowds.

Unlike many royal children, however, Elizabeth and Margaret spent a lot of time with both their parents. The Duke and Duchess visited their children each morning, before they took lessons with their governesses, and at the end of the day they would play cards and have pillow fights until it was time for bed. "In those days we lived in an ivory tower," Crawfie wrote later, "removed from the real world." But the ivory tower could not last. There was a royal storm brewing outside which was set to change their lives forever.

Princess Elizabeth stands in front of her miniature house in the gardens of the Royal Lodge. It was given to her by the people of Wales.

Chapter 2

Heir to the throne

The year Elizabeth turned ten, the family spent Christmas together. King George V was clearly very ill and died a month later. Elizabeth went to his funeral at Windsor Castle, dressed in a new black coat and velvet beret, clutching her mother's hand as the coffin was lowered into the Royal Vault.

George V's funeral procession in London, 1936

At first, little changed in the lives of the princesses. There was now a new king on the throne, their father's brother, King Edward VIII. The public adored him. He had been their golden-haired prince and now he was their young and popular King. But there was a secret hanging over him, kept out of the press and mentioned only in whispers, which was threatening to bring his reign to an abrupt end. Edward was in love with a twice-divorced American woman, Wallis Simpson.

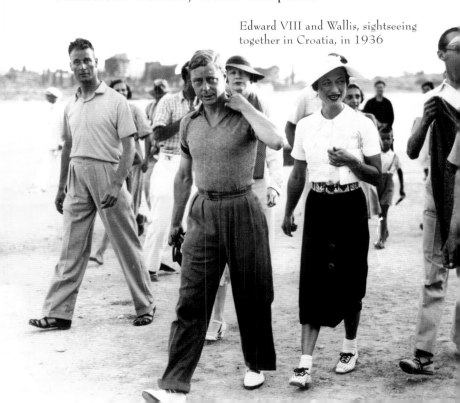

Edward VIII and Wallis, sightseeing together in Croatia, in 1936

Edward VIII broadcasts to the British Empire that he will abdicate.

Divorce was heavily frowned upon then – particularly in royal circles – and it was unthinkable that Edward could marry Wallis and make her his queen.

On October 27, 1936, the newspapers broke the scandal. Given the choice between marrying the woman he loved or remaining King, Edward VIII chose love. When the Duke of York told his mother what had happened he broke down and sobbed like a child. Before the end of the year Edward had abdicated, and Elizabeth's father became King George VI.

The shock was almost too much for the new King. He was a shy man, his shyness made worse by a stammer that made public speaking a nightmare for him, and he had never wanted to be king. Edward's abdication destroyed the brothers' friendship and he was rarely spoken of by Elizabeth's parents again.

For Elizabeth, the realization that she might one day become Queen came gradually. According to her other grandmother, Lady Strathmore, Princess Elizabeth prayed nightly for a brother to take her place as next in line to the throne.

The royal family gather on the balcony of Buckingham Palace after the Coronation ceremony.

"When our father became King," Princess Margaret recalled, "I said to her, 'Does that mean you're going to be Queen?' She replied, 'Yes, I suppose it does.' She didn't mention it again."

Buckingham Palace in 1937 – the flag is flying to show the royal family is in residence.

Any sense of private life was now over. The family moved to Buckingham Palace, where crowds gathered daily outside the railings, hoping to catch a glimpse of them. But for the princesses, it was fun too. "People need bicycles in this place," Elizabeth declared, and Margaret would often ride her tricycle up and down the long palace corridors.

The princesses could no longer take walks in the park or play with the children next-door, but they loved the gardens at Buckingham Palace.

Elizabeth's mother soon made the palace rooms as homely as possible. Elizabeth had a sitting-room of her own, while their schoolroom looked out over the palace gardens. The King set up the children's rocking-horses outside his study so he could hear them play as he worked.

Elizabeth no longer referred to her parents as Mummy and Papa, but spoke of them as the King and Queen. The Queen also insisted on adding a 'touch of majesty' to the nursery, which involved their meals being served by two footmen in scarlet uniform.

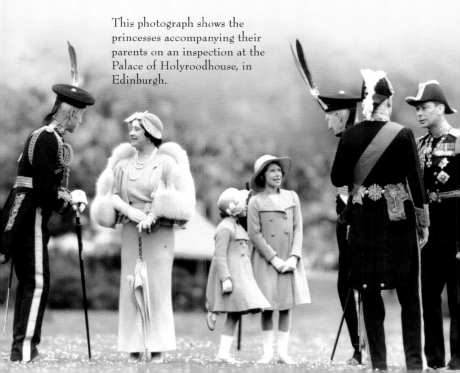

This photograph shows the princesses accompanying their parents on an inspection at the Palace of Holyroodhouse, in Edinburgh.

Outside Buckingham Palace, Princesses Elizabeth and Margaret watch
a regiment being presented with a new flag, known as a standard.

The princesses' lives were now surrounded
by pomp and ceremony, which soon seemed
normal to them. They were attended by a
swarm of staff, and there were also endless
formal occasions. At the State Opening of
Parliament, the princesses watched as their
parents put on their crowns and sat on thrones.

Now that Elizabeth was heir to the throne,
her parents began to take her education more
seriously. She was taught Latin, European
history and the history of the monarchy.

Here you can see Princess Elizabeth as a Girl Guide and Princess Margaret as a Brownie.

Elizabeth also began to join her parents when diplomats and foreign heads of state were visiting.

So that they could still mix with 'ordinary' children, there was a meeting of Girl Guides and Brownies at Buckingham Palace every Wednesday, although all the children involved were also from privileged backgrounds. Elizabeth was described by her cousin, Patricia Mountbatten, as "nice, easy to deal with, you'd want her as your best friend." Already, there was something different about her though. "For instance, she couldn't burst into tears. If she hurt her knee she knew she must try not to cry."

In many ways, Elizabeth was a country girl at heart. She adored her family's weekend trips to Windsor and the summer holidays spent at Balmoral Castle in Scotland. At twelve, she told her riding teacher that if she hadn't been a princess, "I'd like to be a lady living in the country with lots of horses and dogs."

Princess Elizabeth and her father both shared a passion for horses.

Elizabeth remained fascinated by life outside the royal bubble. Years later, when having her portrait painted in the Yellow Drawing Room in Buckingham Palace, she recalled how she had spent hours in the room as a child, looking out of the windows. "I loved watching the people and the cars... They all seemed so busy. I used to wonder what they were doing and where they were all going, and what they thought about outside the Palace."

In 1939, the royal family spent the summer as usual at Balmoral, but their holiday was brought to an abrupt end when the King was summoned to London. He was swiftly followed by the Queen. A few days later, it was announced that Great Britain was at war with Germany.

The first tragedy to strike Elizabeth was the sinking of a battleship, *Royal Oak*, in which 800 sailors died. At Christmas, the princesses were reunited with their parents, but Elizabeth felt guilty about enjoying herself. "Perhaps we were too happy," she wrote to Crawfie. "I kept thinking of those sailors and what Christmas must have been like in their homes."

As German troops swept across Europe, the country was faced with the terrifying threat of invasion. The children and Crawfie were evacuated to Windsor Castle, where they were to stay for five years. The King and Queen remained in London during the day, even as the bombs began to fall, determined to share the dangers faced by their people.

The King and Queen visit a bombed area of the East End of London, in April 1941.

Princess Elizabeth makes her first radio broadcast, alongside her sister Margaret, in 1940. The speech was addressed to all the children of the Commonwealth, many of whom had been sent away during the war.

As part of the war effort, the princesses collected tinfoil, rolled bandages and knitted socks for the forces, and Elizabeth made her first radio broadcast. Despite the mayhem and chaos that surrounded them, the princesses were protected at the Castle, and Elizabeth loved being surrounded by a sense of history. One of Elizabeth's friends described it as having, "a happy family atmosphere."

But Elizabeth was longing for more freedom and the chance to 'do her bit' for the war effort as her friends were. Her father would not allow it. He felt very protective, and as Elizabeth grew older, she found his protectiveness frustrating. "I ought to do as other girls do," she said.

Instead, she spent her time being groomed for her future as Queen, which included meeting any important visitors who came to stay. When Eleanor Roosevelt, wife of the US President, visited in 1942, she described the sixteen-year-old Elizabeth as, "quite serious with a great deal of character and personality. She asked me a number of questions about life in the United States and they were serious questions."

The same year, Elizabeth also inspected a regiment for the first time, which she found "a bit frightening... but it was not as bad as I expected it to be."

In the spring of 1945, just before her nineteenth birthday, she was at last allowed 'out' to join the Auxiliary Territorial Service. For perhaps the only time in her life, she was able to work alongside ordinary people, learning to drive and mend a car.

Dressed in her ATS uniform, Princess Elizabeth tinkers with an engine of a car as she does her mechanical training during the war.

At first, Elizabeth felt shy, but she soon started to talk to the other girls, who were all very interested to meet her. "Quite striking," one girl wrote in her diary at the time, "short pretty brown crisp curly hair. Lovely grey-blue eyes, and an extremely charming smile, and she uses lipstick!"

Elizabeth's experience of mixing with other girls was short-lived. The course came to an end, and soon after, so did the war. As everyone celebrated, Elizabeth and Margaret slipped out of the palace and mingled with the crowds, unrecognized. Years later, Elizabeth remembered, "lines of people linking arms and walking down Whitehall, and all of us were swept along by tides of happiness and relief." The end of the war was also to mark the end of Elizabeth's seclusion, and her girlhood.

Thousands of Londoners gather outside Buckingham Palace to celebrate the end of the war in Europe.

Chapter 3

Love & marriage

Princess Elizabeth and Prince Philip
on honeymoon, in November 1947

Princess Elizabeth first met Prince Philip
of Greece when she was just thirteen, and
he eighteen, at the Royal Naval College at
Dartmouth, where Philip was training as a cadet.
Philip was tall and handsome, with blond hair
and striking features. For Elizabeth, it was a case
of love at first sight.

Philip spent much of the war fighting at sea,
but he saw Elizabeth whenever he was on leave
in London. In 1944, Queen Mary had confided
to an old friend that Elizabeth and Philip had,

"been in love for the past eighteen months. In fact longer, I think… But the King and Queen… want her to see more of the world before committing herself." Queen Mary also admitted that it seemed as if Elizabeth had made up her mind. "There's something very steadfast and determined in her – like her father."

When Prince Philip proposed at Balmoral in 1946, Elizabeth instantly accepted. The King, however, couldn't bear the thought that 'us four' were already to be parted. He made Elizabeth promise that nothing would be official until her twenty-first birthday, and that first the family would go on a tour together, to South Africa.

Princess Elizabeth plays deck games with the crew during the royal family's trip to South Africa.

South Africa was Elizabeth's first experience of the British Commonwealth, the countries that made up, or had once been part of, the British Empire. She had her twenty-first birthday on tour, and marked it with a speech, dedicated to all the people of the Commonwealth. "It is very simple," she said. "I declare before you all that my whole life… shall be devoted to your service and the service of our great Imperial family to which we all belong…" Elizabeth read the words with real earnestness and sincerity, bringing, it was said, "a lump into millions of throats."

On their return, the engagement was announced and they married on a dark November day. Elizabeth wore a fairy-princess dress in ivory silk covered with white roses sewn from pearls. Wedding presents and royalty came from all over the world and for a week there were rounds of parties – a splash of gaiety in the drab post-war world.

Princess Elizabeth and Prince Philip, in his naval uniform, at Buckingham Palace on their wedding day

George VI was deeply moved by the wedding service. While Elizabeth was on honeymoon, he wrote to tell her how he felt.

> I was so proud of you... but when I handed your hand to the Archbishop I felt that I had lost something very precious... do remember that your old home is still yours & do come back to it as much & as often as possible. I can see that you are sublimely happy with Philip which is right but don't forget us is the wish of Your ever loving & devoted Papa.

Crowds line the streets to watch the wedding procession.

Elizabeth and Philip smile for the cameras on their way back from an official engagement.

Elizabeth and Philip, now known as the Duke and Duchess of Edinburgh, returned home from honeymoon to take up their public duties. They visited Paris on an official tour, where they were a great success, described by one onlooker as a divine couple.

In November 1948, Elizabeth gave birth to their first child, HRH Prince Charles Philip Arthur George. When the announcement was made, a huge crowd gathered outside the palace, and the cheering lasted until after midnight.

A few months later, Elizabeth and Philip were able to move into their new home, Clarence House, where they were extremely happy. Philip helped to give his new wife confidence. "She was marvellous at doing her duties," one of her ladies-in-waiting recalled, but "she really was agonizingly shy."

Philip, however, was longing to go back to sea and that year they went out to Malta, where Philip was posted aboard HMS *Chequers*. The baby was left behind with his nannies and grandparents, just as Elizabeth had been left as a baby by her own parents.

Princess Elizabeth gazes at her month-old son.

Princess Elizabeth visits her husband, the Duke of Edinburgh, in Malta in 1949, where the Duke was stationed with the Royal Navy.

In Malta, Elizabeth was able to lead an almost ordinary life, as a naval officer's wife. There was no press to put on a show for, and instead she could go shopping or out to the hairdressers. "They were so relaxed and free, coming and going as they pleased..." recalled a member of their staff. "I think it was their happiest time."

But, after two years, the King's health began to fail. Elizabeth and Philip had to return to England to take on some of his duties. By now, they had two children, Charles and Anne. This wasn't allowed to interfere with Elizabeth's royal duties, however. In 1951, it was decided that the Edinburghs should go on a tour of Australia and New Zealand, in the place of the King and Queen. They were to stop off first in Kenya, to stay at a lodge they had been given as a wedding present.

The King went with them to the airport. Before they left, he said to Bobo, a trusted servant, "Look after the Princess for me." Six days later, he was dead, of a heart attack in his sleep. He was only fifty-six. Elizabeth had left the country a princess. She would return to it as Queen.

King George VI, with hand raised, waves goodbye to his daughter.

Chapter 4

Head of State

Elizabeth, now Queen Elizabeth II,
arriving back from Kenya

On the flight back from Kenya, Elizabeth
appeared calm to those around her,
although one member of staff saw her get up
once or twice and return to her seat, looking
as if she'd been crying. The change in her and
Philip's position was immediate. Gone was their
independence or any sense of freedom. It was
time to take up the reins of duty.

Her grandmother, Queen Mary, came to see her shortly after she arrived home, and met her with a curtsey. "Her old Grannie and subject must be the first to kiss Her hand," she said, much to Elizabeth's dismay.

Still in shock over her father's death, Elizabeth had no time to grieve. The following morning she had to go to the meeting of her Accession Council, where she had formally to declare herself Queen.

"My heart is too full for me to say more to you today than that I shall always work as my father did," she said simply. On the way back in the car with Philip, she finally broke down and sobbed.

But Elizabeth was also helped out of her sadness by her new role. "Mummy and Margaret have the biggest grief to bear, for their future must seem very blank, while I have a job and a family to think of," Elizabeth wrote. She was enjoying her new responsibilities and looking ahead to her Coronation in Westminster Abbey when she would be publicly crowned Queen. There would be celebrations across the nation, from village carnivals to street parties.

As the Coronation date drew near, Elizabeth rehearsed her lines, with sheets pinned to her shoulders so she could get used to the cumbersome robes she would have to wear.

On the day itself, crowds lined the streets, cheering despite the drizzling rain. Elizabeth, in a white satin dress with a red velvet train, waved to them all on her way to the Abbey, a radiant smile on her face. In front of millions of television viewers, the Archbishop presented the public with their new Queen. The congregation roared, "God Save Queen Elizabeth".

The whole ceremony had an ancient air, filled with slow and stately movement, sparkling jewels and solemn vows. For Elizabeth, it was a spiritual rite of passage, as she dedicated her life to that of her people.

Just five months after the coronation, Elizabeth and Philip set out on a six-month tour of the Commonwealth. Elizabeth was to travel more than any other monarch in history. She and Philip frequently sailed aboard the royal yacht, *Britannia*, furnished inside to look like a country house at sea. Here, the royal family could entertain heads of state as well as relaxing after a long day.

Elizabeth took her role as Head of the Commonwealth seriously, but the tours were often long and tiring, and fraught with risk. In 1961, five days before she was due to sail to Ghana, in Africa, two bombs exploded in the capital, Accra. But Elizabeth insisted on going, determined to help keep the country within the Commonwealth, as it was becoming increasingly close to Communist Russia. "She loves her duty and means to be a Queen and not a puppet," the Prime Minister wrote in his diary.

Even at home, the Queen's work never ceased.

The Queen and Prince Philip on their tour of Ghana, driving through the dusty streets to greet the people.

From the beginning, state papers were delivered to her daily in leather-covered boxes. She studied them carefully, and was quick to catch out her Prime Ministers at their weekly meetings if they hadn't read their briefs. One Prime Minster, Harold Macmillan, wrote, "I was astonished at Her Majesty's grasp of all the details."

There was one side of the job that Elizabeth did find a struggle – public speaking. Her honesty meant she found it difficult to say anything she didn't believe and she always read her speeches, which made them sound less spontaneous. A naturally shy person, public occasions were something the Queen did as her duty, rather than a thing to be enjoyed.

As she grew into her role of Queen, a gap was opening up, between her public image, serious and dignified, and Elizabeth's private self. "When she smiles, the whole face comes to life," a relation said. "She loves a good laugh – I've seen the Queen laugh till the tears ran down her face…" One of her fashion advisers described how, "The woman I see is full of jokes... and only too ready to laugh at anything – particularly herself. If only people could see her as she is."

As time passed, Elizabeth found there were great shifts in the public's attitude to the monarchy. She became subject to criticism in the press, from articles abroad claiming she didn't smile enough on state visits, to uproar at home over the amount of money spent on the royal family. Nor was there a time when she could take a day off from being Queen. As a way to relax, she pursued her other interests when she could – country walks, breeding gundogs and her real passion, breeding racehorses. She has been amazingly successful at it, her horses having won nearly all the important races.

The Queen with her first classic racehorse winner at Epsom, in 1957

The Queen was surprised and touched by the crowds that gathered for her Silver Jubilee, in 1977. It was a difficult time for the country, with rising unemployment and little money to spare for celebrations. But, in spite of everything, it was one of the high points of her reign.

There were bonfires and street parties, and hundreds of ordinary people lined the streets to see her as she toured the country. "She could not believe that people had that much affection for her as a person," said her domestic chaplain, "and she was embarrassed and at the same time terribly touched by it all."

The Queen wanted to mark her Jubilee by meeting as many people as possible. Here she greets people on the streets of Camberwell, London.

Elizabeth visited Northern Ireland in her Jubilee year, even though the violence there between Catholics and Protestants put her life in danger. "We said we're going to Ulster," she told her Private Secretary, "and it would be a great pity not to."

The Queen had come to represent something – a symbol of continuity, a focus for the nation, an upholder of the values of courage and decency. And this is what had brought people out of their homes and onto the streets, just to catch a glimpse of her.

At a street party in Belfast, Northern Ireland, during the Queen's Silver Jubilee, children wave the Union Jack flag as a sign of loyalty to the Queen.

Chapter 5

Family strife

Elizabeth couldn't help but be an absent mother. Her tours of the Commonwealth meant she had been away for much of Charles and Anne's childhood, often over birthdays and once over Christmas, too. When at home, though, she kept an hour for the children in the morning and another at bath time. When Charles caught chickenpox, she was unable to see him because of the risk of infection. But, as soon as he had recovered, she refused invitations so she could be with him. Philip, too, made sure he was there to read and play with the children at bedtime.

In 1960, Elizabeth gave birth to another child, Prince Andrew, followed by Prince Edward four years later. "Goodness what fun it is to have a baby in the house again!" she told a friend after Edward was born. "He is a great joy to us all…"

Elizabeth always struggled to protect her children from the press, but her advisers were worried that the monarchy was starting to seem old-fashioned and out of touch. In 1969, for the first time, television cameras were allowed behind the scenes to follow the royal family for a year.

The film showed a happy, wholesome and united family, portraying the royals as ordinary human beings. But there was danger too, as the film made the public more intrigued than ever about the family's personal lives.

By the 1970s, the family was growing apart. Charles had joined the navy, Anne was married, and the younger two were away at school. They were talking less and only really meeting for formal occasions.

A family portrait taken on holiday at Balmoral, Scotland

Prince Charles kisses his bride on the balcony of Buckingham Palace, in front of cheering crowds.

Then, in 1981, Charles was married, to Lady Diana Spencer. The wedding was portrayed as a fairy-tale match on the television, as was Prince Andrew's wedding to Sarah Ferguson in 1986.

The way the newspapers reported the monarchy was also beginning to change. Instead of surrounding them with respect and a sense of mystery, people were being given endless details about every aspect of their lives. The royals had been admired for representing an ideal family, but as their personal lives unravelled in the late 1980s, the press began to turn.

They reported on the rocky relationships within the marriages of the younger royals. If the royal family didn't uphold standards, what was it for?

Things did not get better. The Queen described 1992 as her *'annus horribilis'*, the Latin for 'horrible year'. The announcement that Prince Andrew was to separate from his wife was swiftly followed by Princess Anne's divorce. In June, a book was published detailing the unhappy marriage of Charles and Diana. In November that year, a fire broke out at Windsor Castle, the Queen's childhood home. No one was killed, but the fire caused terrible damage. The Queen was devastated.

Smoke and flames flood the night sky above Windsor Castle. It took nine hours to bring the fire under control.

At first, people reacted sympathetically, but there was an uproar when it was suggested the public should pay for the repair. Then, in December, it was announced that Charles and Diana were to separate.

The Queen responded to the criticism. The monarchy decided to begin paying tax, like the rest of the public, and Buckingham Palace was opened to the public, to help pay for the repairs to Windsor Castle. But while there was still a great deal of respect for the Queen, and a recognition of how well she did her job, the criticism did not go away. Some newspapers painted her as a cold and unfeeling mother and as being out of touch with the public. Through it all, the Queen carried on, doing her job as she had always done – reading and signing papers, giving speeches, meeting people, visiting and touring. "The Queen's strength," said one of her aides, "is that she doesn't change very much."

Then tragedy struck. On August 31, 1997, Princess Diana was killed in a car crash in Paris. The nation went into shock, followed by a public outpouring of grief never seen before. People came in their thousands to lay flowers outside Kensington Palace, where she had lived, and waited for hours to sign books with messages of love and remembrance.

The Queen was staying at Balmoral in Scotland at the time, and remained there, looking after Charles and Diana's children, Prince William and

The Queen and Prince Philip look at the tributes left for Diana outside Buckingham Palace.

Prince Harry. But the public's grief quickly turned to anger, the Queen's absence from London seen as evidence of her uncaring attitude to Diana. The newspapers demanded the Union flag be flown at Buckingham Palace at half-mast, as a sign of respect to Diana, and that the Queen come and talk to her people.

Diana's brother, Earl Spencer, Prince William and Harry and their father, Prince Charles, at Diana's funeral

In the face of such anger, the Queen was forced to comply. She left Balmoral for London, and as she arrived at the palace, the crowds began to clap. That evening, Elizabeth went on television to speak about Diana. "I for one," she said, "believe that there are lessons to be drawn from her life and from the extraordinary and moving reaction to her death." To survive, the monarchy was going to have to change.

Chapter 6

A job for life

The Queen's approach to change had always been cautious, unwilling to abandon the traditions and customs followed by her own parents. Following Diana's death, however, she seemed more open to suggestion and ready to take on some of the ways Diana had performed her role – being more informal, and having more direct contact with ordinary people, in ordinary places.

Here the Queen makes an informal visit to a primary school in Northern Ireland.

Her days were arranged differently, so she spent more time talking to the people she met on her visits. She was shown keeping up with the times, smiling more for the cameras and speaking more about current concerns.

The new-style 'modern' monarchy was put to the test in 1999, when Australia held a vote to decide if, as a member of the Commonwealth, it wanted to keep the Queen as Head of State. Everyone expected Australia to vote to become a republic, but instead just over half the Australian people voted to keep the Queen.

The Queen accepts flowers from schoolgirls in Canberra, Australia, in 2000. The Queen has made sixteen visits to Australia during her reign.

The royal family's popularity was given a further boost, as attention shifted away from the Queen's children to her grandchildren. In 2000, Prince William, like many other teenagers leaving school, went on a gap year, doing charitable work both in the UK and abroad. Images of the prince cleaning toilets on a project in South America put across the idea of the royal family as increasingly in touch with the lives of ordinary people.

Prince William, on his gap year in Chile, makes a wooden rubbish bin for the local villagers.

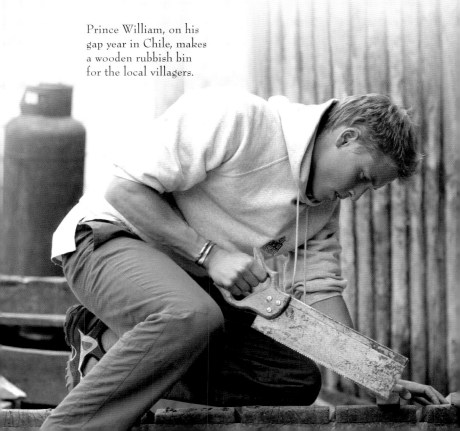

The year of the Queen's Golden Jubilee, 2002, celebrated her fifty years on the throne. But it began with two great losses for the Queen – the death of her sister, Princess Margaret, in February, followed by that of her mother less than two months later, at the age of 101.

The Queen Mother with her two daughters on her 100th birthday

Two hundred thousand people came to pay their respects to the Queen Mother, walking past her coffin as it lay in state in Westminster Hall. Despite this profound show of loyalty and affection, many newspapers predicted that the Golden Jubilee would be a failure, claiming that the British public was no longer interested in the monarchy.

They were proved wrong, as hundreds of thousands thronged to fêtes up and down the country, while a million people came to the parade in the Mall, in London.

With the wedding of Prince William and Catherine Middleton in April 2011, the royal family seemed once again to be riding a wave of popularity. Over 24 million people tuned in to watch the wedding on television in the UK, with millions more watching around the world.

Away from the pomp and finery of grand royal occasions, the Queen, now in her eighties, continues to work hard at her job. At a time of life when most people are settled in their retirement, she shows the same energy and determination in fulfilling her duties as she has always done. In May 2011, she made a historic visit to the Republic of Ireland, the first British monarch to visit the country since 1911.

Prince William and his bride, now the Duchess of Cambridge, smile and wave at the crowds from the balcony at Buckingham Palace.

Despite the risk from republican terrorists, the Queen spent her four-day visit commemorating the lives that had been lost in the struggles between the two countries, cementing a new era of friendship between them.

The Queen has described her role as "a job for life". A lonely one at times, but helped, she has said, by her husband, whom she has called "my strength and stay all these years".

Through all the ups and downs the monarchy has faced, the Queen has never stopped working. Her oath to serve her country, which she took at the age of twenty-five, was a heartfelt one, holding true over fifty years later.

2012 is the year of the Queen's Diamond Jubilee, celebrating her sixty years on the throne. It makes her the second-longest serving monarch in British history. Her reign has seen twelve British Prime Ministers come and go and she remains a popular Head of State to fifteen Commonwealth countries. Whatever the future holds for the monarchy, the Queen's reign will be remembered for her dignity and her devotion to the role. As Sir Winston Churchill, her very first Prime Minister, said of her, "I became conscious of the Royal resolve to serve as well as rule, and indeed to rule by serving."

The Queen in April 2011,
attending a service at
Windsor Castle

ACKNOWLEDGEMENTS

© akg-images p9; © **Camera Press** p1 (Lord Snowdon), p44 (John Bulmer); © **Corbis** spine (Hulton-Deutsch Collection), p15 (Hulton-Deutsch Collection), p56 (PAUL MCERLANE/epa); © **Getty Images** pp2-3 (Scott E Barbour/Image Bank), p5, p6, p7, p8 (Popperfoto), p10, p12, p13(tr) (Popperfoto), p13(b), p14, p16, p17, p20, p21, p22, p23, p24 (Time & Life Pictures), p25 (Gamma-Keystone), p28, p30 (Popperfoto), p31 (SSPL), p32, p33 (Popperfoto), p34 (via Gamma-Keystone), p35, p37 (Gamma-Keystone), p39 (Popperfoto), p40 (AFP), p46, p47, p50 (Lichfield), p55, p58 (Tim Graham), p63; © **Press Association Images** p11 (AP/AP), p18 (Topham/ Topham Picturepoint), p19 (PA/PA Archive), p27 (/S&G Barratts/EMPICS Archive), p43 (PA/PA Archive), p51 (PA/PA Archive), pp60-1 (Chris Ison/ PA Wire); © **Rex Features** p52, p54, p59 (Mike Forster/Daily Mail); © **Topfoto.co.uk** p36 (AP), p38 (2005), p48 (2002, Topham Picturepoint), p57 (Topham/PA); © **Victoria & Albert Museum, London** front cover (Queen Elizabeth II in Coronation Robes, photo Cecil Beaton (1904-80). Photograph. UK, 1953).

Please note some of the black and white images in the book have been digitally tinted by Usborne.

Internet links

You can find out more about the Queen by going to the Usborne Quicklinks website at **www.usborne-quicklinks.com** and typing the keywords "the queen".

Edited by Jane Chisholm

Digital manipulation by Keith Furnival

With thanks to Ruth King for her help with picture research